ARIZONA
COYOTES

BY DAVID J. CLARKE

Book design by Maggie Villaume
Cover design by Maggie Villaume

Photographs ©: Jeff Roberson/AP Images, cover; Jason Franson/The Canadian Press/AP Images, 4–5, 7, 8; Holly Stein/AP Images, 10–11; Ray Giguere/The Canadian Press/AP Images, 13; Phil Snell/The Canadian Press/AP Images, 15; Mike Fiala/AP Images, 16–17; Danny Moloshok/AP Images, 19; Ross D. Franklin/AP Images, 21, 24–25; Gene J. Puskar/AP Images, 23; Nam Y. Huh/AP Images, 27; Jack Dempsey/AP Images, 28

Press Box Books, an imprint of Press Room Editions.

ISBN
978-1-63494-672-8 (library bound)
978-1-63494-696-4 (paperback)
978-1-63494-742-8 (epub)
978-1-63494-720-6 (hosted ebook)

Library of Congress Control Number: 2022919239

Distributed by North Star Editions, Inc.
2297 Waters Drive
Mendota Heights, MN 55120
www.northstareditions.com

Printed in the United States of America
Mankato, MN
082023

ABOUT THE AUTHOR

David J. Clarke is a freelance sportswriter. Originally from Helena, Montana, he now lives in Savannah, Georgia, with his golden retriever, Gus.

TABLE OF CONTENTS

1

The Coyotes scored 14 goals in their four-game playoff series against the Nashville Predators in 2020.

MOVING
ON

Fans had waited a long time to see the Arizona Coyotes back in the National Hockey League (NHL) postseason. Finally, after eight years, they got their wish in 2020.

The COVID-19 pandemic had shut down the NHL season. It finally resumed in August. An expanded playoff format helped Arizona qualify. But the Western Conference playoffs were held entirely in Edmonton, Alberta. There was no one in the stands. Yet miles away in Arizona, Coyotes fans were on the edges of their seats.

The Coyotes opened against the favored Nashville Predators. Arizona took a 2–1 series lead into Game 4. A win would clinch the best-of-five series. With 32 seconds left, the Coyotes were on their way. Then Nashville's Filip Forsberg scored a late goal to tie the game 3–3. It was time for the Coyotes to dig deep.

The Coyotes created a scoring chance five minutes into overtime. Arizona winger Vinnie Hinostroza took a pass along the wall. As he turned to face the net, he had time to shoot. But he also spotted

Darcy Kuemper had a .933 save percentage in the series against the Predators.

teammate Brad Richardson on the other side of the ice. Richardson was cutting toward the net.

Brad Richardson (15) celebrates his overtime goal against the Predators.

Hinostroza snaked a pass through the defense. Richardson went down to a knee to try to punch it on goal. Nashville goalie Juuse Saros made a diving save. But the play wasn't over. The puck bounced off a Nashville defender and fell right back to Richardson. Saros was out of position. Richardson jabbed his stick at the puck and poked it in.

The game was over. The Coyotes had won the series. In the next round, they faced the Colorado Avalanche. Colorado came out on top. But Arizona's win over Nashville had finally ended the team's long wait for a playoff-series victory.

• DARCY DOES IT

The biggest reason the Coyotes beat the Predators was goaltender Darcy Kuemper. Nashville outshot the Coyotes in all four games. Kuemper stopped 40 of 43 shots to win Game 1. In Game 3 he turned away 39 of 40. But Game 4 was his best performance. Kuemper made 49 saves in the 4–3 win.

2

Alex Zhamnov scored more than 20 goals in all four seasons he played in Winnipeg.

WINNIPEG YEARS

The Coyotes began playing in 1972. But they were far from the desert of Arizona. And they didn't even play in the NHL. The team was founded as the Winnipeg Jets. And it played in the rival World Hockey Association (WHA).

The Jets were one of the WHA's best teams. They were led by stars like future Hall of Fame forward Bobby Hull. Three times the Jets hoisted the Avco World Trophy.

That was the WHA's version of the Stanley Cup. However, by the late 1970s the league wasn't making enough money. It was forced to merge with the NHL. Four teams from the WHA joined the NHL in 1979 as part of the deal. The Jets were one of them.

Life wasn't as easy in the NHL. In their first two seasons, the Jets won only 29 out of 160 games. That changed when the team picked center Dale Hawerchuk in the 1981 draft. The 18-year-old rookie became

•EUROPEAN INFLUENCE

Top European players are everywhere in the NHL now. That wasn't the case in the 1970s. However, the Jets featured several European players. Swedish forwards Anders Hedberg and Ulf Nilsson were both high scorers. The Jets even had a Swedish captain in defenseman Lars-Erik Sjöberg.

Dale Hawerchuk tries to score against the Edmonton Oilers during a
playoff game in 1990.

the youngest player to score 100 points
in a season. "Ducky" also led the Jets to
the playoffs.

Hawerchuk continued to shine throughout the 1980s. He topped 100 points six times. And he was soon joined by other standouts like center Thomas Steen and defenseman Randy Carlyle. The Jets became a regular playoff team during the 1980s.

Winning in the postseason was tougher. The Jets won only two playoff series in the 1980s. And they never made it past the second round.

Hawerchuk was traded in 1990. The Jets needed a new offensive star. And they got one in 1992–93. Finnish forward Teemu Selänne lit up the NHL right away. Selänne scored a rookie record 76 goals. The old mark had been 53.

Teemu Selänne tallied 306 points in 231 games with Winnipeg.

Selänne was soon joined by goalie Nikolai Khabibulin. The Russian shot-stopper earned the nickname the "Bulin Wall" for his play. But neither superstar could save the team in Winnipeg.

3

Keith Tkachuk's 52 goals led the NHL in the 1996–97 season.

PHOENIX RISING

The Jets made the playoffs 11 times in 17 NHL seasons. But they were struggling in Winnipeg. The city was one of the smallest in the NHL. By 1995–96, it was clear the Manitoba capital could no longer support the team.

The Jets were sold and moved to Arizona. They debuted as the Phoenix Coyotes in 1996–97. Teemu Selänne didn't make the move. He had been traded to the

Mighty Ducks of Anaheim. Instead, the Coyotes relied on forwards Keith Tkachuk and Jeremy Roenick. They led Phoenix to the playoffs for four straight years. But like the old Jets, postseason wins were in short supply. The Coyotes lost in the first round each season.

In 2000–01, the Coyotes began to go downhill. They made the playoffs only once for the next eight seasons. The highlight of that stretch was a new

KACHINA

When the team moved to Phoenix, its new coyote logo was inspired by a kachina. These dolls are part of the traditions of the Pueblo and Hopi nations, which have made the area their home since long before Arizona became a state. The team moved away from the logo in the early 2000s. But it stayed popular. The Coyotes brought the kachina logo back in 2021–22.

Jeremy Roenick played six of his 20 NHL seasons with the Coyotes.

arena that the team opened in 2003 in

Glendale, Arizona.

Even the greatest player of all time

couldn't turn the team around. No player

had scored more NHL points than Wayne Gretzky. And he had been part owner of the Coyotes since 2001. In 2005–06, he became the head coach. But Phoenix never won more than 38 games in any of the four seasons Gretzky coached. Even worse, the Coyotes also went bankrupt. The NHL had to step in and take control of the team.

Gretzky stepped down in 2009. Dave Tippett replaced him the next year. Tippett led the Coyotes to an amazing turnaround. Phoenix won 50 games despite not scoring many goals. Captain Shane Doan led the Coyotes with 55 points. But Phoenix allowed only 202 goals. That was the third fewest in the league.

Shane Doan sends a Detroit Red Wings player into the boards during a 2010 playoff game.

The playoffs remained an issue. In a seven-game battle, Phoenix fell in the first round to the Detroit Red Wings. However, a longer run was just around the corner.

SHANE DOAN

Shane Doan was never the flashiest player. But he could do everything on the ice.

The center recorded the most points in Coyotes history. But it took Doan a while to find the net. In his first four seasons he scored just 22 goals. Then in his fifth year alone he put up 26. He went on to score at least 20 in each of the next eight seasons.

Doan was also one of the most respected leaders in the league. He captained the Coyotes from 2003 until his retirement in 2017.

That leadership was reflected in his two career NHL awards. Doan won the King Clancy Memorial Trophy in 2009–10. The Clancy is given to the player who is both a team leader and a humanitarian off the ice. Two years later he won the Mark Messier Leadership Award.

Shane Doan played all
21 of his NHL seasons with
the Jets and Coyotes.

4

Phoenix fans cheer on goalie Mike Smith during the 2012 playoffs.

LOST IN THE
DESERT

Phoenix reached the playoffs again in 2010–11. But it didn't advance past the first round. A year later the Coyotes won 42 games. That was enough to win the Pacific Division. It was the team's first division title since joining the NHL.

Shane Doan led the way along with veteran forwards Ray Whitney and Radim Vrbata. Young defensemen Keith Yandle and

Oliver Ekman-Larsson contributed at both ends. Mike Smith was one of the best goalies in the NHL that year.

Phoenix met the powerhouse Chicago Blackhawks in the first round of the playoffs. The first five games went to overtime. Coyotes forward Mikkel Boedker scored two overtime winners as Phoenix took a 3–2 series lead. The series went back to Chicago for Game 6. Smith shut the door with a 4–0 shutout. That secured the team's first playoff-series win since 1987.

Phoenix thumped the Nashville Predators 4–1 in the second round. But the Coyotes lost in the conference finals to the Los Angeles Kings in five games.

Mikkel Boedker celebrates scoring an overtime goal in the 2012 playoffs.

After that, the team dealt with a number of changes. The Coyotes were still owned by the NHL. They had nearly

Nick Schmaltz broke out with 59 points in 2021–22.

moved several times. In 2013, new owners
stepped in and kept the team in Arizona. A
year later they changed the team's name

from "Phoenix" to "Arizona." That didn't affect the performance on the ice, though. The Coyotes kept losing. Fans stopped coming to games. For years, the Coyotes were near the bottom in NHL attendance.

A short playoff run in 2020 didn't help much. In 2021–22, Arizona won only 25 games. But the team had young star centers in Clayton Keller and Nick Schmaltz. Fans hoped another playoff run wasn't far away.

RING OF HONOR

Leighton Accardo loved the Arizona Coyotes. But at age seven, she was diagnosed with cancer. She died in 2020 at the age of nine. In 2021, the Coyotes added Leighton to their Ring of Honor. It celebrates the most important people in the team's history. Leighton was the eighth person inducted. But she was the first who wasn't a former player.

ARIZONA COYOTES
QUICK STATS

TEAM HISTORY: Winnipeg Jets (1972–96), Phoenix Coyotes (1996–2014), Arizona Coyotes (2014–)

STANLEY CUP CHAMPIONSHIPS: 0

KEY COACHES:

- Jim Schoenfeld (1997–99): 74 wins, 66 losses, 24 ties

- Bobby Francis (1999–2004): 165 wins, 144 losses, 60 ties, 21 overtime losses

- Dave Tippett (2009–17): 282 wins, 257 losses, 83 overtime losses

HOME ARENA: Mullett Arena (Tempe, AZ)

MOST CAREER POINTS: Shane Doan (972)

MOST CAREER GOALS: Shane Doan (402)

MOST CAREER ASSISTS: Shane Doan (570)

MOST CAREER SHUTOUTS: Mike Smith (22)

Stats are accurate through the 2021–22 season.

GLOSSARY

BANKRUPT
Unable to pay ones' debts due to lack of money.

CAPTAIN
A team's leader.

DRAFT
An event that allows teams to choose new players coming into the league.

HUMANITARIAN
A person who wants to help other people.

MERGE
Join together.

PANDEMIC
An outbreak of a disease that affects much or all of the world.

ROOKIE
A first-year player.

VETERAN
A player who has spent several years in a league.

TO LEARN
MORE

BOOKS

Davidson, B. Keith. *NHL*. New York: Crabtree Publishing, 2022.

Doeden, Matt. *G.O.A.T. Hockey Teams*. Minneapolis: Lerner Publications, 2021.

Duling, Kaitlyn. *Women in Hockey*. Lake Elmo, MN: Focus Readers, 2020.

MORE INFORMATION

To learn more about the Arizona Coyotes, go to **pressboxbooks.com/AllAccess**.

These links are routinely monitored and updated to provide the most current information available.

INDEX